NON-ALCOHOLIC FATTY LIVER DISEASE COOKBOOK

Delicious Recipes for a Healthier Liver and Body

SAVANNAH GRACE

Copyright © 2023 by Savannah Grace.

All rights reserved. No part of this book may be reproduced in any form or by any electronic or mechanical means including information storage and retrieval systems, without permission in writing from the publisher, except by a reviewer who may quote brief passages in a review.

This book is a work of nonfiction. The names, characters, places, and incidents are products of the author's imagination or are used fictitiously. Any resemblance to actual events, locales, or persons, living or dead, is entirely coincidental.

TABLE OF CONTENT

INTRODUCTION 7

    Overview of Liver Disease 10

    What is liver disease?.. 10

    Which are the most common forms of liver disease?....11

    What liver disease symptoms and causes are common?13

    Typical signs of liver illness include the following: 14

    How can liver disease be prevented and treated? 16

CHAPTER 1 19

    Foods to Eat and Avoid on a Liver Disease Diet 19

    Benefits of following a liver disease diet for beginners (or seniors).. 23

CHAPTER 2 26

    Healthy shopping ingredients or lists for a liver disease diet.. 29

    The complications of liver disease, if the right diet isn't adopted... 35

CHAPTER 3 39

Meal planning for liver disease diet, and it's benefits for proper management 39

7-day liver disease meal plan. 41

    Day 1 41

    Day 2 42

    Day 3 43

    Day 4 43

    Day 5 44

    Day 6 44

    Day 7 45

CHAPTER 4 46

Liver disease breakfast recipes 46

    1. Oatmeal with Fresh Berries and Walnuts 46

    2. Scrambled Eggs with Spinach and Cheese** 47

    3. Whole Wheat Pancakes with Fresh Strawberries and Honey 49

    4. Muesli with Low-Fat Milk and Blueberries 51

    5. Omelet with Mushrooms and Cheese 53

6. French Toast with Fresh Raspberries and Maple Syrup 54

7. Smoothie Bowl with Low-Fat Yogurt, Banana, Berries, and Flax Seeds 56

8. Whole Wheat Bagel with Cream Cheese and Smoked Salmon 58

9. Chia Yogurt with Coconut and Mango 59

10. Mushroom Omelette with Cheese and Spinach 60

Lunch recipes for Liver disease 62

1. Tabbouleh Stuffed Pepper 62

2. Indian Chickpea and Artichoke Saute 64

3. Quinoa Salad with Fresh Vegetables 66

4. Soba Noodles and Vegetables 68

5. Sesame Pork Tacos 70

7. Chicken and Vegetable Stir-Fry with Brown Rice** 72

8. Mediterranean Salad with Tuna and White Beans 75

9. Turkey and Cheese Wrap with Lettuce and Tomato . 76

10. Vegetable and Bean Chili with Whole Wheat Tortilla Chips 78

Dinner Recipes for Liver disease 81

1. Salmon with Quinoa and Broccoli 81

2. Vegetable Lasagna with Low-Fat Cheese 83

3. Roasted Chicken with Roasted Potatoes and Asparagus 86

4. Beef and Vegetable Stew with Barley 88

5. Baked Cod with Lemon and Herbs 90

6. Vegetable Curry with Chickpeas and Spinach 92

7. Turkey Meatloaf with Mashed Cauliflower and Green Beans 94

8. Greek Salad with Grilled Chicken and Pita Bread.... 97

9. Vegetable and Tofu Stir-Fry with Brown Rice 99

10. Vegetable and Cheese Quesadillas 102

CONCLUSION 105

INTRODUCTION

Mr. Okeke was a retired teacher, sixty-five years old, who enjoyed eating pounded yam, egusi soup, and fried plantains. His smile was as large as his belly, and he loved to read newspapers and watch TV during the day. He was frequently visited by his wife, two kids, and four grandchildren.

During a routine check-up at the hospital one day, he was told some unfavorable news. His physician informed him those years of consuming excessive amounts of fat and sugar had resulted in liver damage. He warned that unless Mr. Okeke changed his food and way of life, he would run into major problems.

Mr. Okeke felt terrified and shocked. He did not want to give up his food or his life because he loved both so much. He enquired as to how he can control or reverse his illness from the doctor. In addition to giving him a list of things to consume and foods to avoid, the doctor also suggested that he increase his water and exercise intake. If Mr. Okeke did as he was told, he may potentially improve the condition of his liver.

Mr. Okeke returned home filled with rage and depression. He detested the concept of sweating and panting, as much as the idea of eating bland, monotonous food. He made the decision to disregard the doctor's advice and carry on as normal. He rationalized to himself that he was too old to change and that a joyful death was preferable to a miserable one.

He devoured more pounded yam, egusi soup, and fried plantains throughout the course of the following few weeks. In addition, he watched more TV, slept more, and consumed more soft beverages and palm wine. Though his liver illness was getting worse, he disregarded the signals and felt lethargic and exhausted. He assured his wife and boys that the doctor was overstating his condition and that he was OK.

He fell on the ground one day while watching a football game. He was taken to the hospital right away after his wife called for help. He discovered there that he required a liver transplant as his liver had failed. He also discovered that he had kidney issues, high blood pressure, and diabetes. He came to the realization that he had endangered his life by making a grave error.

He pleaded with the physician to locate him a donor and to save his life. The physician explained that while finding a match was difficult, he would try. He claimed that in addition to having to adhere to a rigorous food and medicine schedule, Mr. Okeke had to wait a very long period. He warned Mr. Okeke that he would not survive if he did not alter his actions and attitude.

Mr. Okeke was regretful and embarrassed. He wished he had taken better care of his liver and that he had paid attention to the doctor sooner. He wished he had consumed less sugar and fat and more fruits and veggies. He wished he had increased his water and exercise intake. He regretted not prioritizing his health over his enjoyment.

He prayed to God asking for assistance in finding a donor and for a second opportunity. He committed to living a happier and healthier life and to changing his ways. He wished he could see his wife, sons, and grandchildren once more and that it wouldn't be too late.

He hoped for the best and waited for a miracle.

Overview of Liver Disease

Hundreds of bodily processes, including metabolism, energy storage, detoxification, and blood filtration, are carried out by the liver, an essential organ. But the liver can also be impacted by a number of illnesses that harm its structure and function and cause major health issues. I will define liver illness, list its primary forms, discuss its common causes and symptoms, and discuss treatment and prevention options for liver disease in this essay.

What is liver disease?

A generic term used to describe any illness affecting the liver and preventing it from functioning correctly is "liver disease." Acute (short-term) and chronic (long-term) liver diseases can vary in severity. Depending on the kind and stage of the disease, liver disease might result in cirrhosis, inflammation, scarring, or liver failure. Other organs and systems in the body, including the brain, kidneys, pancreas, and immune system, can also be impacted by liver illness.

Which are the most common forms of liver disease?

Liver illness comes in various forms, however some of the most prevalent ones are as follows:

Hepatitis: A viral infection is typically the cause of hepatitis, an inflammation of the liver. Hepatitis caused by viruses comes in five varieties: A, B, C, D, and E. Other substances, including alcohol, narcotics, poisons, and autoimmune diseases, can also result in hepatitis. Hepatitis can be acute or chronic, and it can cause cancer, cirrhosis, or damage to the liver.

Fatty liver disease: When fat builds up in the liver cells, it can lead to an enlargement and malfunction of the liver cells. Obesity, diabetes, high cholesterol, and alcohol abuse are all risk factors for fatty liver disease. Fatty liver disease comes in two flavors: alcoholic fatty liver disease (AFLD) and nonalcoholic fatty liver disease (NAFLD). Cirrhosis, fibrosis, inflammation, and liver failure can develop as a result of fatty liver disease.

Cirrhosis: This disease causes the liver's structural integrity and function to be lost as scar tissue replaces the original liver tissue. Chronic hepatitis, fatty liver disease, alcohol misuse, and other conditions can all lead to cirrhosis. Hepatic encephalopathy, bleeding varices, ascites, portal hypertension, and liver cancer are among the problems that can arise from cirrhosis.

Liver cancer: This type of cancerous growth starts out in the bile ducts or liver cells. One can have primary liver cancer, which begins in the liver, or secondary liver cancer, which spreads to other organs. Aflatoxin exposure, cirrhosis, hereditary factors, and chronic hepatitis are all potential causes of liver cancer. Ascites, weight loss, jaundice, and stomach pain are some of the symptoms that liver cancer can produce.

A potentially fatal condition known as liver failure occurs when the liver is unable to produce enough liver cells, which causes waste products and toxins to build up in the blood. Both acute and chronic liver failure are possible (gradual). A drug overdose, liver damage, cirrhosis, liver cancer, and severe hepatitis are among the conditions that can cause liver failure. Jaundice, hemorrhage, edema, confusion, and coma are among the symptoms of liver failure.

What liver disease symptoms and causes are common?

Depending on the kind and stage of the disease, there are many causes and signs of liver disease. But among the frequent reasons of liver disease are:

Viral infections: Hepatitis A, B, C, D, and E are examples of viruses that can infect the liver and result in inflammation, damage, or malignancy.

Abuse of alcohol: Drinking too much alcohol can harm liver cells and result in cirrhosis, hepatitis, fatty liver disease, or liver failure.

Diabetes and obesity: Excess weight and elevated blood sugar levels can contribute to cirrhosis, fatty liver disease, and inflammation in the liver.

Drugs and toxins: Hepatitis, cirrhosis, or liver failure can be brought on by some drugs, herbal supplements, or chemicals that damage the liver.

Autoimmune disorders: A number of illnesses, including primary sclerosing cholangitis, autoimmune hepatitis, and primary biliary cholangitis, can trigger an immune response against the liver that results in cirrhosis, inflammation, and scarring.

Genetic disorders: A number of hereditary conditions, including hemochromatosis, Wilson's disease, and alpha-1 antitrypsin deficiency, can impair liver metabolism and result in iron, copper, or protein buildup in the liver, which can cause damage, cirrhosis, or cancer.

Typical signs of liver illness include the following:

Jaundice: Jaundice is a yellowing of the skin and eyes brought on by an accumulation of bilirubin in the blood, which is a waste product of the breakdown of red blood cells. Jaundice may be a symptom of malignancy, cirrhosis, hepatitis, or liver disease.

Abdominal discomfort and swelling: This condition can be brought on by an infection, an enlarged liver, a buildup of fluid in the belly (ascites), portal hypertension, cirrhosis, or liver failure.

Dark urine and pale stools: Hepatitis, cirrhosis, cancer, and liver disease can all result in decreased bilirubin and bile excretion.

Itching: Liver damage, cirrhosis, hepatitis, or cancer can all result in the buildup of bile salts in the skin.

Fatigue and weakness: The liver's decreased ability to produce energy and proteins, as well as the buildup of toxins and waste products in the blood as a result of liver damage, hepatitis, cirrhosis, or liver failure, can all contribute to fatigue and weakness.

Nausea and vomiting: liver damage, hepatitis, cirrhosis, or liver failure can all result in an accumulation of waste products and toxins in the blood, which can lead to nausea and vomiting. It can also result from the liver's poor ability to digest and absorb food.

Hepatitis, cirrhosis, liver damage, and bleeding: These conditions can result in increased pressure in the portal vein, bleeding, and bruises.

Depressive symptoms: These conditions can be brought on by the buildup of toxins in the blood, such as ammonia, which can impair brain function.

Liver damage: These conditions can result in liver damage, hepatitis, cirrhosis, and liver failure can cause depression and bleeding. Hepatic encephalopathy is the term for this illness.

How can liver disease be prevented and treated?

The kind and stage of liver disease determine the course of treatment and prevention. But a few broad actions that can aid in the management and prevention of liver disease include:

Immunization: Immunization offers protection against viral hepatitis and liver cancer-causing hepatitis A and B. Individuals who have a chronic liver illness, travel, or work in healthcare settings who are at risk of exposure should consider being vaccinated.

Screening and testing: These methods can assist in the early detection of liver disease, before it results in permanent damage or problems. People who are at risk of liver disease, such as those who use drugs or alcohol, have a family history of the condition, have chronic hepatitis, have diabetes, are obese, or have other medical conditions, should get screenings and tests.

- A change in lifestyle can help lower risk factors and enhance the prognosis of liver disease. Changes in lifestyle include abstaining from alcohol, cutting back on sugar, managing blood pressure, maintaining a healthy weight, getting regular exercise, and staying away from pollutants and narcotics.

Medications: Medications can help address the underlying cause or the symptoms of liver disease. Medications for hepatitis, autoimmune hepatitis, chelators for hemochromatosis or Wilson's disease, diuretics for ascites, lactulose for hepatic encephalopathy, and opioids for liver discomfort are among the medications available.

Surgery: Surgery can aid in the removal or replacement of the liver's diseased or damaged tissue. Surgery can involve shunt surgery for portal hypertension, liver transplantation for liver failure, or liver resection for liver malignancy.

Supportive care: People with liver disease can live better and manage their problems with the aid of supportive care.

Blood transfusions for bleeding, dietary supplements for malnourishment, or palliative care for liver disease in the last stages are examples of supportive care.

CHAPTER 1
Foods to Eat and Avoid on a Liver Disease Diet

The liver is an essential organ that carries out numerous bodily processes, including blood filtration, detoxification, and metabolism. But a number of illnesses can also damage the liver and make it less able to function properly. Nonalcoholic fatty liver disease (NAFLD), a disorder in which the liver cells retain extra fat, is one of the most prevalent liver illnesses. Diabetes, obesity, elevated cholesterol, and other conditions can all contribute to NAFLD. If NAFLD is not treated, it may worsen and cause scarring, cirrhosis, inflammation, or liver failure.

One of the main things that can affect how NAFLD and other liver illnesses start and progress is diet. In order to lower risk factors, enhance liver function, and avoid consequences, a balanced diet can help prevent and treat liver disease. Generally speaking, a diet low in fat should follow these guidelines:

Increase your intake of fruits and vegetables. They are a good source of fiber, vitamins, minerals, and antioxidants that can help shield the liver from oxidative stress, inflammation, and damage. Additionally, while blood pressure, cholesterol, and blood sugar are risk factors for NAFLD, fruits and vegetables can help lower these levels. Berries, citrus fruits, apples, grapes, broccoli, carrots, beets, spinach, kale, and grapes are a few fruits and vegetables that are particularly good for the liver.

Consume additional whole grains and legumes: Legumes, whole grains, and other plant-based foods are excellent providers of fiber, protein, and complex carbohydrates that can help control blood sugar, cholesterol, and hunger. Important minerals that are necessary for liver function, such as iron, zinc, magnesium, and B vitamins, can also be found in whole grains and legumes. Oats, barley, quinoa, brown rice, lentils, beans, and soy are a few healthy grains and legumes that are beneficial to the liver.

Eat more lean meats and fish: These foods are excellent providers of high-quality protein, which is necessary for liver health and repair. Omega-3 fatty acids are anti-inflammatory and can help prevent or minimize the buildup of liver fat. They can also be found in fish and lean foods. Salmon, tuna, sardines, mackerel, chicken, turkey, and eggs are a few fish and lean meats that are beneficial to the liver.

- Increase your intake of nuts and seeds. They are a good source of fiber, protein, and healthy fats that can help decrease triglycerides and cholesterol and enhance liver function. Additionally, antioxidants, vitamin E, and selenium found in nuts and seeds can help shield the liver from oxidative stress and damage. Nuts and seeds beneficial to the liver include walnuts, almonds, pistachios, sunflower, flax, and chia seeds.

Eat more herbs and spices: In addition to providing antioxidants, anti-inflammatory, and antimicrobial qualities that can help prevent or treat liver disease, spices and herbs can enhance flavor and variety in a diet. Turmeric, ginger, garlic, cinnamon, rosemary, thyme, and oregano are a few herbs and spices that are beneficial to the liver.

- Refrain from drinking alcohol or use it sparingly: Alcohol can lead to cirrhosis, liver failure, scarring, inflammation, and fat buildup, which are all major causes of liver damage. Additionally, alcohol can alter liver metabolism and function and raise the risk of liver cancer. Thus, alcohol should be avoided or used in moderation by those who have liver disease, or they should abide by their doctor's recommendations.

- Steer clear of or use added sugars sparingly: Added sugars include table sugar, honey, syrups, and sweeteners, which are added to meals and beverages during processing or preparation. The risk factors for NAFLD, such as blood sugar, insulin, and triglycerides, can all rise with added sweets. Additionally, added sugars may exacerbate liver disease by causing an excess of calories, weight gain, and obesity. Therefore, foods and beverages that are naturally sweetened or unsweetened should be chosen by those who have liver disease, and added sugars should be avoided or limited.

- Refined carbs (white bread, white rice, white pasta, and pastries) should be avoided or consumed in moderation. These are carbohydrates that have been processed and depleted of their fiber, vitamins, and minerals. Refined carbs can raise insulin, triglycerides, blood sugar, and lead to obesity, weight gain, and excess calories in a manner similar to that of added sugars.

Hence, it is recommended that individuals with liver disease pick diets that are manufactured with whole grains or other complex carbs and avoid or limit processed carbohydrates.

Limit or stay away from trans and saturated fats: Butter, lard, margarine, and shortening are examples of solid fats that are saturated and trans fats. Triglycerides and cholesterol are raised by trans and saturated fats, and these are risk factors for non-alcoholic fatty liver disease (NAFLD). Additionally, oxidative stress, inflammation, and liver damage can be caused by trans and saturated fats. Thus, foods high in unsaturated fats, such avocado, canola, or olive oil, should be preferred by those suffering from liver disease over meals high in saturated or trans fats, which should be avoided or consumed in moderation.

Benefits of following a liver disease diet for beginners (or seniors).

For beginners or seniors seeking to enhance their liver health and avoid or cure liver disease, adhering to a liver disease diet can offer numerous advantages. A few of the main advantages are:

- Reducing the risk of liver damage: Restricting or avoiding foods and beverages that can damage the liver, such as alcohol, refined carbs, added sugars, and saturated and trans fats, is possible with a liver disease diet. These drugs may result in cirrhosis, inflammation, fat buildup, scarring, or liver failure. A liver disease diet can lessen the chance of liver damage and its consequences by eliminating or reducing them.

- Improving liver function: A diet for liver disease can assist in giving the liver the proper nourishment and vital nutrients it needs to carry out its processes, including blood filtering, metabolism, and detoxification. In addition, blood sugar, cholesterol, and triglycerides—all critical for liver function—can be regulated with the aid of a diet plan for liver illness. A diet for liver disease can assist enhance liver function and shield it from overwork by giving it enough nourishment and vital nutrients.

Hepatitis, cirrhosis, nonalcoholic fatty liver disease (NAFLD), and liver cancer are among the conditions that a liver disease diet can aid in preventing or treating. The primary symptom of nonalcoholic fatty liver disease (NAFLD) can be lessened with the aid of a diet for liver disease. Inflammation and oxidative stress are factors in the development of liver disease, and a food plan for liver disease can help reduce them. The signs and consequences of liver illness, such as jaundice, edema and soreness in the abdomen, itching, weakness and exhaustion, bleeding and bruises, confusion, and mood swings, can also be avoided or lessened with the aid of a diet plan for liver disease.

A healthy and balanced diet that minimizes or eliminates alcohol, added sugars, refined carbs, saturated and trans fats, and contains more fruits, vegetables, whole grains, legumes, fish, lean meats, nuts, seeds, and spices is known as a liver disease diet. Beginners and seniors alike can enhance their liver health and prevent or treat liver disease with the use of a liver disease diet.

CHAPTER 2

How to keep to a diet for liver disease

Eating a diet high in items that support liver function and limiting or avoiding foods that can damage the liver is the foundation of a liver disease diet. Following a liver disease diet can be done in the following simple ways:

Consume a greater number of fruits and vegetables, particularly those high in fiber, vitamins, minerals, and antioxidants. These may aid in defending your liver against oxidative stress, inflammation, and harm. Broccoli, carrots, beets, apples, grapes, citrus fruits, berries, and spinach are a few examples.

- Incorporate more whole grains and legumes into your diet, including soy, quinoa, brown rice, barley, lentils, and beans. These can help control your blood sugar, cholesterol, and hunger. They are also rich sources of protein, fiber, and complex carbohydrates. In addition, they may offer vital nutrients that are critical to the health of your liver, like iron, zinc, magnesium, and B vitamins.

Consume greater quantities of fish and lean meats, including eggs, chicken, turkey, tuna, sardines, and mackerel. You need high-quality protein for your liver to function and heal, and these are good sources of it. They can also supply omega-3 fatty acids, which have anti-inflammatory properties and can lessen or stop the buildup of liver fat.

Consume a greater variety of nuts and seeds, including chia, flax, walnut, almond, and pistachio seeds to name a few. They are abundant in fiber, protein, and healthy fats that can help decrease triglycerides and cholesterol while also enhancing liver function. Additionally, they may offer vitamin E, selenium, and antioxidants that can guard your liver from oxidative stress and damage.

Consume a greater number of herbs and spices, including oregano, cinnamon, ginger, turmeric, lemongrass, and rosemary. They offer anti-inflammatory, anti-microbial, and antioxidant qualities that can help prevent or treat liver disease in addition to bringing taste and diversity to your diet.

As one of the primary causes of liver disease, avoid or use alcohol sparingly.

Cirrhosis, fat buildup, scarring, inflammation, and liver failure can all be brought on by alcohol. It may potentially worsen liver cancer risk and disrupt liver metabolism and function.

Avoid or use sugar additives sparingly, including syrups, sweeteners, honey, and table sugar. These put you at risk for nonalcoholic fatty liver disease (NAFLD) by raising your triglycerides, blood sugar, and insulin levels. Additionally, they may compound your liver illness by causing you to consume more calories than you need, gain weight, and become obese.

Refined carbs, such as white rice, white bread, white spaghetti, and pastries, should be avoided or consumed in moderation. In addition to raising blood sugar, insulin, and triglycerides, these can also have the same consequences as additional sweets by causing an increase in calories, weight gain, and obesity.

- Steer clear of or use shortening, butter, lard, margarine, and other foods high in saturated and trans fats.

As risk factors for NAFLD, these can raise your triglycerides and cholesterol levels. Inflammation, oxidative stress, and liver damage can also be caused by these.

Healthy shopping ingredients or lists for a liver disease diet

An eating plan specifically designed to address and prevent liver disease, particularly nonalcoholic fatty liver disease (NAFLD), is known as a liver disease diet. A diet for liver disease consists of foods that are healthy for the liver and minimizes or stays away from those that can cause liver damage.

- Fruits: Packed with antioxidants, vitamins, minerals, and fiber, fruits can shield the liver from damage, inflammation, and oxidative stress. Fruits including berries, citrus fruits, apples, grapes, kiwis, and lemons are particularly good for the liver.

- Vegetables: Rich in antioxidants, vitamins, minerals, and fiber, vegetables can help reduce blood pressure, cholesterol, and blood sugar—all of which are risk factors for non-alcoholic fatty liver disease (NAFLD).

Broccoli, carrots, beets, cabbage, spinach, kale, and broccoli are a few vegetables that are beneficial to the liver.

- Whole grains: Rich in fiber, protein, and complex carbs, whole grains can help control blood sugar, cholesterol, and appetite. Additionally, they can supply vital minerals that are crucial for liver function, like iron, zinc, magnesium, and B vitamins. Oatmeal, barley, quinoa, brown rice, and buckwheat are a few whole grains that are beneficial to the liver.

- Legumes: Rich in fiber, protein, and complex carbohydrates, legumes can help control blood sugar, cholesterol, and hunger. Additionally, they can supply vital minerals that are crucial for liver function, like iron, zinc, magnesium, and B vitamins. Lentils, beans, chickpeas, and soy are a few legumes that are beneficial to the liver.

- Fish: Fish are an excellent source of high-quality protein, which is necessary for the maintenance and healing of the liver. Additionally, they may offer omega-3 fatty acids, which have anti-inflammatory properties and may help stop or lessen the buildup of liver fat.

Salmon, tuna, sardines, mackerel, and herring are a few seafood that are beneficial for the liver.

- Lean meats: High-quality protein, which is necessary for liver function and repair, can also be found in lean meats. Additionally, they can supply selenium, zinc, and iron—all of which are critical for liver function. Lean meats like chicken, turkey, pork, and eggs are beneficial for the liver.

- Nuts: Packed with fiber, protein, and good fats, nuts can help decrease triglycerides and cholesterol while also enhancing liver function. Additionally, they may offer vitamin E, selenium, and antioxidants that help shield the liver from oxidative stress and damage. Nuts including cashews, pistachios, walnuts, and almonds are beneficial to the liver.

- Seeds: Rich in fiber, protein, and healthy fats, seeds can help decrease triglycerides and cholesterol while also enhancing liver function. Additionally, they may offer vitamin E, selenium, and antioxidants that help shield the liver from oxidative stress and damage. Sunflower, flax, chia, and pumpkin seeds are a few types of seeds that are beneficial to the liver.

- Olive oil: Rich in antioxidants and a healthy fat, olive oil can help reduce inflammation and oxidative stress while also supporting better liver function. Additionally, olive oil can enhance insulin sensitivity and prevent or lessen the buildup of liver fat, all of which are critical for the prevention or treatment of NAFLD.

- Avocado: This is another type of healthy fat that can help reduce oxidative stress and inflammation while also supporting better liver function. In addition, avocado can enhance insulin sensitivity and prevent or lessen the buildup of liver fat, all of which are critical for the prevention or treatment of NAFLD.

- Spices: In addition to offering taste and diversity to a diet, spices also have anti-inflammatory, anti-microbial, and antioxidant qualities that can help prevent or treat liver disease. The following spices are beneficial to the liver: cumin, ginger, garlic, cinnamon, and turmeric.

- Herbs: In addition to offering taste and diversity to the diet, herbs also include anti-inflammatory, anti-microbial, and antioxidant qualities that can aid in the prevention or treatment of liver disease. Herbs such as basil, cilantro, parsley, rosemary, thyme, oregano, lemongrass, and lavender are beneficial to the liver.

- Low-fat dairy: Probiotics, calcium, and protein are included in low-fat dairy products, and these nutrients can help with digestion and liver function. Lowering triglycerides and cholesterol, two risk factors for NAFLD, can also be achieved with low-fat dairy products. Low-fat Greek yogurt, low-fat kefir, and skim milk are a few dairy products that are beneficial to the liver.

- Green tea: Rich in antioxidants, polyphenols, and catechins, green tea may help shield the liver from oxidative stress, inflammation, and damage. In addition, green tea can enhance insulin sensitivity and reduce the buildup of liver fat, both of which are critical for the prevention or treatment of NAFLD.

- Coffee: This additional beverage can help shield the liver from oxidative stress, inflammation, and damage since it contains antioxidants, caffeine, and chlorogenic acid. Additionally, coffee can aid in lowering liver enzymes, which are indicators of damage and inflammation in the liver. Additionally, coffee can lessen or prevent the chance of developing liver cancer and cirrhosis.

- Water: Since it helps your body rid itself of waste materials and toxins, water is the ideal beverage to consume for your liver. In addition, water helps keep your body's fluid balance and hydrate your cells and tissues. Dehydration can also be treated or prevented with water, and it can lead to headaches, dizziness, and exhaustion.

- Dark chocolate: Rich in flavonoids, polyphenols, and antioxidants, dark chocolate can shield the liver from oxidative stress, inflammation, and damage. Additionally beneficial to liver health are reduced blood pressure and enhanced hepatic blood flow, both of which can be achieved with dark chocolate. But since dark chocolate also includes calories and sugar, which can be bad for the liver if ingested in excess, it should only be eaten in moderation.

- Oatmeal: Rich in soluble fiber, beta-glucan, and antioxidants, oatmeal is a breakfast food that can help decrease triglycerides and cholesterol while also enhancing liver function. In addition, oatmeal can aid in blood sugar and appetite regulation, both of which are critical for the management or prevention of NAFLD.

- Berries: Rich in antioxidants, anthocyanins, and polyphenols, berries are a snack food that can help shield the liver from damage, inflammation, and oxidative stress. Additionally, as blood sugar and cholesterol are risk factors for NAFLD, berries can help lower these levels. Cranberries, blueberries, raspberries, and strawberries are a few berries that are beneficial to the liver.

- Grapefruit: This citrus fruit has antioxidants called naringenin and naringenin, which can help shield the liver from damage, inflammation, and oxidative stress. In addition, grapefruit has been shown to reduce the buildup of liver fat and enhance insulin sensitivity, both of which are critical for the management or prevention of NAFLD.

The complications of liver disease, if the right diet isn't adopted.

Liver disease is a dangerous ailment that can impact not only the liver but also other body organs and systems. Numerous conditions, including viruses, alcoholism, medications, toxins, obesity, diabetes, autoimmune diseases, and genetic disorders, can result in liver disease. Symptoms of liver illness include jaundice, dark urine and pale feces, itching, weariness and weakness, bleeding and bruises, nausea and vomiting, confusion, and mood swings.

Liver disease can deteriorate a person's health and quality of life if the proper diet is not followed. It can also cause other difficulties. Following are a few potential liver disease side effects:

Ascites: Ascites is a condition in which there is an accumulation of fluid in the abdominal cavity as a result of elevated pressure in the portal vein, which transports blood from the liver to the digestive organs. Infection, renal failure, breathing problems, and pain in the abdomen are all possible effects of ascites.

- Variceal bleeding: This condition is caused by the esophageal or stomach enlarged veins rupturing as a result of elevated portal vein pressure. Blood vomiting, dark stools, shock, or even death can result from variceal hemorrhage.

Hepatic encephalopathy: This condition is characterized by a decrease in brain function brought on by the buildup of toxins, such as ammonia, in the blood that the liver is unable to filter. Confusion, mood swings, insomnia, coma, or even death are possible outcomes of hepatic encephalopathy.

- Hepatorenal syndrome: This condition is the decline in kidney function brought on by the advanced liver disease's decreased blood supply to the kidneys. Reduced urine output, edema, elevated blood pressure, and even mortality are possible outcomes of hepatorenal syndrome.

The abnormal growth of cells in the liver that can infiltrate or spread to other regions of the body is known as liver cancer. Aflatoxin exposure, cirrhosis, hereditary factors, and chronic hepatitis are all potential causes of liver cancer. Ascites, weight loss, jaundice, and stomach pain are some of the symptoms that liver cancer can produce.

A potentially fatal condition known as liver failure occurs when the liver is unable to produce enough enzymes to break down waste products and poisons into the circulation. Both acute and chronic liver failure are possible (gradual). A drug overdose, liver damage, cirrhosis, liver cancer, and severe hepatitis are among the conditions that can cause liver failure. Jaundice, hemorrhage, edema, confusion, and coma are among the symptoms of liver failure.

Because these liver disease complications can significantly influence an individual's health and well-being, it's critical to adopt a balanced diet that can both prevent and treat liver disease. In addition to limiting or avoiding alcohol, added sugars, refined carbs, saturated and trans fats, and fish and lean meats, a healthy diet for liver disease should include more fruits and vegetables, whole grains and legumes, nuts and seeds, spices, and herbs.

CHAPTER 3

Meal planning for liver disease diet, and it's benefits for proper management

The act of organizing and cooking meals that are appropriate for those with liver disease is known as meal planning for liver disease diet. Planning meals can assist those who suffer from liver disease in:

- Provide for their dietary needs and guard against malnutrition, which can deteriorate liver function and raise the possibility of problems.

- Restrict their calorie intake and keep a healthy weight, as this can lessen the inflammatory response and formation of liver fat.

- Steer clear of or consume in moderation foods and beverages that might damage the liver, such as alcohol, refined carbs, added sweets, and saturated and trans fats.

Incorporate foods and beverages including fruits, vegetables, whole grains, legumes, fish, lean meats, nuts, seeds, spices, and herbs that are known to protect and enhance the liver.

- Handle their liver disease symptoms and consequences, including jaundice, edema and pain in the abdomen, itching, weakness and exhaustion, nausea and vomiting, bleeding and bruises, confusion, and mood swings.

Those who have liver illness might use the following procedures to prepare meals for their diet:

- Speak with their physician and nutritionist to establish specific dietary requirements and objectives based on their medical history, preferred foods, medications, and the type and stage of their liver disease.

-- When you go grocery shopping, make a list of the ingredients and amounts needed for the dinner and follow it.

- Try to prepare and cook as many meals as you can at home. Avoid deep-frying, frying, and overusing oil, butter, or salt. Instead, use healthy cooking techniques like baking, grilling, steaming, or boiling.

- To prevent overindulging in food or missing meals, portion and serve meals in accordance with the suggested serving sizes.

- Avoid or consume in moderation alcohol, soft drinks, and caffeinated beverages. Instead, drink lots of water and other liquids, such as herbal teas, juices, or smoothies.

- Keep track of and document how meals affect liver function, symptoms and problems, general health and well-being, and modify the menu as necessary.

7-DAY LIVER DISEASE MEAL PLAN.

Day 1

- Breakfast: Oatmeal with fresh berries and walnuts, low-fat Greek yogurt, and green tea

- Snack: Apple slices with almond butter

- Lunch: Spinach salad with grilled chicken, avocado, and sunflower seeds, whole wheat bread, and water

- Snack: Carrot sticks with hummus

- Dinner: Salmon with quinoa and broccoli, fruit salad, and water

Day 2

- Breakfast: Scrambled eggs with spinach and cheese, whole wheat toast, and orange juice

- Snack: Banana with peanut butter

- Lunch: Lentil soup with whole wheat pita bread, cucumber and tomato salad, and water

- Snack: Mixed nuts and dried fruits

- Dinner: Turkey meatballs with brown rice and green beans, low-fat yogurt, and water

Day 3

- Breakfast: Whole wheat pancakes with fresh strawberries and honey, low-fat milk, and coffee

- Snack: Celery sticks with cream cheese

- Lunch: Chicken and vegetable stir-fry with brown rice, fruit smoothie, and water

- Snack: Granola bar and grapes

- Dinner: Vegetable lasagna with low-fat cheese, green salad, and water

Day 4

- Breakfast: Muesli with low-fat milk and blueberries, hard-boiled egg, and herbal tea

- Snack: Pear and cheese

- Lunch: Tuna salad sandwich with whole wheat bread, carrot and apple slaw, and water

- Snack: Popcorn and raisins

- Dinner: Roasted chicken with roasted potatoes and asparagus, apple pie, and water

Day 5

- Breakfast: Omelet with mushrooms and cheese, whole wheat muffin, and grapefruit juice

- Snack: Yogurt and granola

- Lunch: Vegetable and bean chili with whole wheat tortilla chips, green salad, and water

- Snack: Cherry tomatoes and mozzarella cheese

- Dinner: Beef and vegetable stew with barley, whole wheat roll, and water

Day 6

- Breakfast: French toast with fresh raspberries and maple syrup, low-fat milk, and coffee

- Snack: Orange and almonds

- Lunch: Turkey and cheese wrap with whole wheat tortilla, lettuce, tomato, and mustard, vegetable soup, and water

- Snack: Hummus and pita bread

- Dinner: Baked cod with lemon and herbs, couscous and peas, fruit salad, and water

Day 7

- Breakfast: Smoothie bowl with low-fat yogurt, banana, berries, and flax seeds, whole wheat bagel, and green tea

- Snack: Kiwi and pistachios

- Lunch: Pasta salad with chicken, broccoli, and olives, whole wheat bread, and water

- Snack: Peanut butter and jelly sandwich with whole wheat bread

- Dinner: Vegetable curry with chickpeas and spinach, brown rice, low-fat yogurt, and water

CHAPTER 4

LIVER DISEASE BREAKFAST RECIPES

1. Oatmeal with Fresh Berries and Walnuts

Ingredients:

- 1/2 cup of rolled oats

- 1 cup of water or low-fat milk

- A pinch of salt

- 1/4 cup of fresh berries (such as blueberries, raspberries, or strawberries)

- 2 tablespoons of chopped walnuts

- 1 teaspoon of honey (optional)

Preparation:

- In a small saucepan, bring the water or milk and salt to a boil over medium-high heat.

- Add the oats and reduce the heat to low. Simmer, stirring occasionally, for about 15 minutes or until the oats are soft and creamy.

- Transfer the oatmeal to a bowl and top with the berries, walnuts, and honey if desired.

Nutritional Value (per serving):

- Calories: 314

- Fat: 14 g

- Carbohydrates: 43 g

- Fiber: 7 g

- Protein: 10 g

Cooking Time: 20 minutes

2. Scrambled Eggs with Spinach and Cheese**

Ingredients:

- 2 eggs

- 2 tablespoons of low-fat milk

- A pinch of salt and pepper

- 1 teaspoon of olive oil

- 1 cup of fresh spinach, washed and chopped

- 1/4 cup of low-fat cheese, shredded (such as mozzarella, cheddar, or feta)

Preparation:

- In a small bowl, whisk the eggs, milk, salt, and pepper until well combined.

- In a nonstick skillet, heat the oil over medium-high heat. Add the spinach and cook, stirring, for about 5 minutes or until wilted.

- Reduce the heat to low and pour the egg mixture over the spinach. Cook, stirring, for about 10 minutes or until the eggs are set and cooked to your liking.

- Sprinkle the cheese over the eggs and cook for another 5 minutes or until the cheese is melted.

- Serve hot or cold.

Nutritional Value (per serving):

- Calories: 297

- Fat: 20 g

- Carbohydrates: 6 g

- Fiber: 2 g

- Protein: 23 g

Cooking Time: 20 minutes

3. Whole Wheat Pancakes with Fresh Strawberries and Honey

Ingredients:

- 1 cup of whole wheat flour

- 2 teaspoons of baking powder

- A pinch of salt

- 1 cup of low-fat milk

- 1 egg

- 2 tablespoons of vegetable oil

- 1/4 cup of fresh strawberries, sliced

- 2 tablespoons of honey

Preparation:

- In a large bowl, whisk the flour, baking powder, and salt until well combined.

- In a medium bowl, whisk the milk, egg, and oil until well blended.

- Add the wet ingredients to the dry ingredients and stir until just moistened. Do not overmix.

- Heat a lightly greased griddle or skillet over medium-high heat. Drop about 1/4 cup of batter onto the griddle and cook for about 3 minutes or until bubbles form on the surface. Flip and cook for another 3 minutes or until golden brown. Repeat with the remaining batter.

- Serve the pancakes with the strawberries and honey on top.

Nutritional Value (per serving):

- Calories: 349

- Fat: 14 g

- Carbohydrates: 51 g

- Fiber: 6 g

- Protein: 11 g

Cooking Time: 20 minutes

4. Muesli with Low-Fat Milk and Blueberries

Ingredients:

- 1/4 cup of rolled oats

- 2 tablespoons of chopped almonds

- 1 tablespoon of sunflower seeds

- 1 tablespoon of raisins

- 1/4 teaspoon of cinnamon

- 1 cup of low-fat milk

- 1/4 cup of fresh blueberries

Preparation:

- In a small bowl, toss the oats, almonds, sunflower seeds, raisins, and cinnamon until well mixed.

- In a microwave-safe bowl, heat the milk for about 2 minutes or until hot but not boiling.

- Add the oat mixture to the milk and stir well.

- Top with the blueberries and enjoy.

Nutritional Value (per serving):

- Calories: 375

- Fat: 16 g

- Carbohydrates: 49 g

- Fiber: 7 g

- Protein: 15 g

Cooking Time: 10 minutes

5. Omelet with Mushrooms and Cheese

Ingredients:

- 2 eggs

- 2 tablespoons of low-fat milk

- A pinch of salt and pepper

- 1 teaspoon of olive oil

- 1/2 cup of sliced mushrooms

- 1/4 cup of low-fat cheese, shredded (such as mozzarella, cheddar, or feta)

Preparation:

- In a small bowl, whisk the eggs, milk, salt, and pepper until well combined.

- In a nonstick skillet, heat the oil over medium-high heat. Add the mushrooms and cook, stirring, for about 10 minutes or until browned and tender.

- Reduce the heat to low and pour the egg mixture over the mushrooms. Cook, lifting the edges with a spatula, for about 15 minutes or until the eggs are set and cooked to your liking.

- Sprinkle the cheese over the omelet and fold it in half.

- Serve hot or cold.

Nutritional Value (per serving):

- Calories: 295

- Fat: 20 g

- Carbohydrates: 6 g

- Fiber: 1 g

- Protein: 23 g

Cooking Time: 25 minutes

6. French Toast with Fresh Raspberries and Maple Syrup

Ingredients:

- 2 slices of whole wheat bread

- 1 egg

- 1/4 cup of low-fat milk

- A pinch of cinnamon

- 1 teaspoon of butter

- 1/4 cup of fresh raspberries

- 2 tablespoons of maple syrup

Preparation:

- In a shallow dish, whisk the egg, milk, and cinnamon until well blended.

- Dip each slice of bread in the egg mixture, turning to coat both sides.

- In a large skillet, melt the butter over medium-high heat. Cook the bread for about 3 minutes per side or until golden brown.

- Serve the French toast with the raspberries and maple syrup on top.

Nutritional Value (per serving):

- Calories: 367

- Fat: 12 g

- Carbohydrates: 56 g

- Fiber: 6 g

- Protein: 14 g

Cooking Time: 15 minutes

7. Smoothie Bowl with Low-Fat Yogurt, Banana, Berries, and Flax Seeds

Ingredients:

- 1/2 cup of low-fat yogurt

- 1 banana, peeled and sliced

- 1/4 cup of fresh berries (such as blueberries, raspberries, or strawberries)

- 2 tablespoons of flax seeds

- 1/4 cup of granola (optional)

Preparation:

- In a blender, combine the yogurt, banana, berries, and flax seeds and blend until smooth and creamy.

- Transfer the smoothie to a bowl and top with the granola if desired.

- Enjoy with a spoon.

Nutritional Value (per serving):

- Calories: 355

- Fat: 12 g

- Carbohydrates: 55 g

- Fiber: 11 g

- Protein: 13 g

Cooking Time: 10 minutes

8. Whole Wheat Bagel with Cream Cheese and Smoked Salmon

Ingredients:

- 1 whole wheat bagel, sliced in half

- 2 tablespoons of low-fat cream cheese

- 2 ounces of smoked salmon

- 2 slices of tomato

- 2 lettuce leaves

Preparation:

- Toast the bagel halves until lightly browned and crisp.

- Spread the cream cheese evenly over the bagel halves.

- Top with the smoked salmon, tomato, and lettuce.

- Enjoy as a sandwich or open-faced.

Nutritional Value (per serving):

- Calories: 387

- Fat: 13 g

- Carbohydrates: 47 g

- Fiber: 6 g

- Protein: 24 g

Cooking Time: 10 minutes

9. Chia Yogurt with Coconut and Mango

Ingredients:

- 1/4 cup of chia seeds

- 1 cup of low-fat yogurt

- 2 tablespoons of shredded coconut

- 1/4 cup of fresh mango, diced

Preparation:

- In a small bowl, stir the chia seeds and yogurt until well combined.

- Refrigerate for at least 4 hours or overnight to allow the chia seeds to absorb the liquid and form a gel-like texture.

- Sprinkle the coconut and mango over the chia yogurt and enjoy.

Nutritional Value (per serving):

- Calories: 353

- Fat: 16 g

- Carbohydrates: 40 g

- Fiber: 13 g

- Protein: 16 g

Cooking Time: 10 minutes (plus refrigeration time)

10. Mushroom Omelette with Cheese and Spinach

Ingredients:

- 2 eggs

- 2 tablespoons of low-fat milk

- A pinch of salt and pepper

- 1 teaspoon of olive oil

- 1/2 cup of sliced mushrooms

- 1/4 cup of low-fat cheese, shredded (such as mozzarella, cheddar, or feta)

- 1 cup of fresh spinach, washed and chopped

Preparation:

- In a small bowl, whisk the eggs, milk, salt, and pepper until well combined.

- In a nonstick skillet, heat the oil over medium-high heat. Add the mushrooms and cook, stirring, for about 10 minutes or until browned and tender.

- Reduce the heat to low and pour the egg mixture over the mushrooms. Cook, lifting the edges with a spatula, for about 15 minutes or until the eggs are set and cooked to your liking.

- Sprinkle the cheese over the omelet and fold it in half.

- In another skillet, heat some water over high heat and bring it to a boil. Add the spinach and cook, stirring, for about 5 minutes or until wilted and bright green. Drain the spinach and squeeze out the excess water.

- Serve the omelet with the spinach on the side.

Nutritional Value (per serving):

- Calories: 325

- Fat: 20 g

- Carbohydrates: 9 g

- Fiber: 3 g

- Protein: 28 g

Cooking Time: 30 minutes

LUNCH RECIPES FOR LIVER DISEASE

1. Tabbouleh Stuffed Pepper

Ingredients:

- 4 large bell peppers (any color), halved and seeded

- 1 cup of cooked bulgur

- 2 tablespoons of extra virgin olive oil

- 1/4 cup of fresh parsley, chopped

- 2 tablespoons of fresh mint, chopped

- 2 tablespoons of lemon juice

- Salt and pepper to taste

- 1/4 cup of feta cheese, crumbled

Preparation:

- Preheat the oven to 375°F and lightly grease a baking dish.

- In a large bowl, toss the bulgur, olive oil, parsley, mint, lemon juice, salt, and pepper until well combined.

- Spoon the bulgur mixture into the pepper halves and sprinkle the feta cheese on top.

- Place the stuffed peppers in the prepared baking dish and bake for 25 minutes or until the peppers are tender and the filling is heated through.

Nutritional Value (per serving):

- Calories: 232

- Fat: 11 g

- Carbohydrates: 31 g

- Fiber: 8 g

- Protein: 7 g

Cooking Time: 35 minutes

2. Indian Chickpea and Artichoke Saute

Ingredients:

- 2 teaspoons of coconut oil

- 1 onion, chopped

- 2 cloves of garlic, minced

- 1 tablespoon of curry powder

- 1 teaspoon of cumin

- 1/4 teaspoon of salt

- 1/4 teaspoon of cayenne pepper (optional)

- 2 cups of vegetable broth

- 2 cans of chickpeas, drained and rinsed

- 1 can of artichoke hearts, drained and quartered

- 2 tablespoons of fresh cilantro, chopped

- 2 cups of cooked brown rice

Preparation:

- In a large skillet, heat the oil over medium-high heat. Add the onion and garlic and cook, stirring, for about 15 minutes or until soft and golden.

- Stir in the curry powder, cumin, salt, and cayenne pepper if using and cook for another minute, stirring constantly.

- Add the broth, chickpeas, and artichokes and bring to a boil. Reduce the heat and simmer, uncovered, for about 20 minutes or until the sauce is slightly thickened.

- Stir in the cilantro and serve over the rice.

Nutritional Value (per serving):

- Calories: 398

- Fat: 9 g

- Carbohydrates: 68 g

- Fiber: 16 g

- Protein: 16 g

Cooking Time: 40 minutes

3. Quinoa Salad with Fresh Vegetables

Ingredients:

- 1 cup of quinoa, rinsed and drained

- 2 cups of water

- 1/4 teaspoon of salt

- 2 tablespoons of apple cider vinegar

- 1 tablespoon of honey

- 1/4 cup of extra virgin olive oil

- Salt and pepper to taste

- 2 cups of cherry tomatoes, halved

- 1 cucumber, diced

- 1/4 cup of fresh basil, chopped

- 1/4 cup of fresh parsley, chopped

Preparation:

- In a small saucepan, bring the quinoa, water, and salt to a boil over high heat. Reduce the heat and simmer, covered, for about 15 minutes or until the quinoa is fluffy and the water is absorbed. Fluff with a fork and let it cool slightly.

- In a small bowl, whisk the vinegar, honey, olive oil, salt, and pepper until well blended.

- In a large bowl, toss the quinoa, tomatoes, cucumber, basil, and parsley until well combined.

- Drizzle the dressing over the salad and toss to coat.

- Serve cold or at room temperature.

Nutritional Value (per serving):

- Calories: 295

- Fat: 15 g

- Carbohydrates: 37 g

- Fiber: 5 g

- Protein: 7 g

Cooking Time: 25 minutes

4. Soba Noodles and Vegetables

Ingredients:

- 8 ounces of soba noodles

- 2 tablespoons of sesame oil

- 2 tablespoons of soy sauce

- 1 tablespoon of rice vinegar

- 1 teaspoon of honey

- 1/4 teaspoon of red pepper flakes (optional)

- 2 teaspoons of vegetable oil

- 2 cups of broccoli florets

- 1 carrot, peeled and sliced

- 1 red bell pepper, sliced

- 2 green onions, sliced

- 2 tablespoons of sesame seeds, toasted

Preparation:

- Cook the soba noodles according to the package directions, drain, and rinse under cold water.

- In a small bowl, whisk the sesame oil, soy sauce, rice vinegar, honey, and red pepper flakes if using until well blended.

- In a large skillet, heat the vegetable oil over high heat. Add the broccoli, carrot, and bell pepper and stir-fry for about 10 minutes or until crisp-tender.

- Add the noodles and the sauce and toss to combine.

- Sprinkle the green onions and sesame seeds over the noodles and serve.

Nutritional Value (per serving):

- Calories: 342

- Fat: 13 g

- Carbohydrates: 51 g

- Fiber: 5 g

- Protein: 12 g

Cooking Time: 20 minutes

5. Sesame Pork Tacos

Ingredients:

- 1 pound of lean pork tenderloin, cut into thin strips

- 2 tablespoons of low sodium soy sauce

- 1 tablespoon of honey

- 1 tablespoon of sesame oil

- 1 teaspoon of grated ginger

- 1/4 teaspoon of garlic powder

- 8 small corn or whole wheat tortillas

- 2 cups of shredded cabbage

- 1/4 cup of chopped cilantro

- 2 tablespoons of lime juice

- Salt and pepper to taste

Preparation:

- In a medium bowl, toss the pork with the soy sauce, honey, sesame oil, ginger, and garlic powder until well coated. Refrigerate for at least 30 minutes or up to 4 hours.

- Preheat the oven to 375°F and lightly grease a baking sheet.

- Arrange the pork strips in a single layer on the prepared baking sheet and bake for 15 minutes or until cooked through and slightly caramelized.

- In a small bowl, toss the cabbage, cilantro, lime juice, salt, and pepper until well combined.

- Warm the tortillas in the microwave or oven and fill them with the pork and the cabbage slaw.

- Serve with your favorite salsa or hot sauce if desired.

Nutritional Value (per serving):

- Calories: 287

- Fat: 9 g

- Carbohydrates: 32 g

- Fiber: 5 g

- Protein: 23 g

Cooking Time: 45 minutes (plus marinating time)

7. Chicken and Vegetable Stir-Fry with Brown Rice**

Ingredients:

- 1 cup of brown rice

- 2 cups of water

- 1/4 teaspoon of salt

- 1 pound of boneless, skinless chicken breast, cut into thin strips

- 2 tablespoons of low sodium soy sauce

- 1 tablespoon of honey

- 1 tablespoon of cornstarch

- 1/4 teaspoon of red pepper flakes (optional)

- 2 teaspoons of sesame oil

- 2 cups of broccoli florets

- 1 red bell pepper, sliced

- 2 cloves of garlic, minced

- 2 teaspoons of grated ginger

- 2 tablespoons of chopped green onions

Preparation:

- In a small saucepan, bring the rice, water, and salt to a boil over high heat. Reduce the heat and simmer, covered, for about 40 minutes or until the rice is tender and the water is absorbed. Fluff with a fork and keep warm.

- In a medium bowl, toss the chicken with 1 tablespoon of soy sauce, the honey, the cornstarch, and the red pepper flakes if using until well coated.

- In a large skillet, heat the oil over high heat. Add the chicken and cook, stirring, for about 15 minutes or until golden and cooked through. Transfer to a plate and keep warm.

- In the same skillet, add the broccoli, bell pepper, garlic, ginger, and the remaining soy sauce and cook, stirring, for about 10 minutes or until the vegetables are crisp-tender.

- Return the chicken to the skillet and toss to combine.

- Serve the stir-fry over the rice and sprinkle with the green onions.

Nutritional Value (per serving):

- Calories: 386

- Fat: 7 g

- Carbohydrates: 54 g

- Fiber: 5 g

- Protein: 32 g

Cooking Time: 55 minutes

8. Mediterranean Salad with Tuna and White Beans

Ingredients:

- 2 cans of tuna, drained and flaked

- 1 can of white beans, drained and rinsed

- 2 cups of cherry tomatoes, halved

- 1/4 cup of sliced black olives

- 1/4 cup of chopped fresh parsley

- 2 tablespoons of extra virgin olive oil

- 2 tablespoons of lemon juice

- Salt and pepper to taste

- 4 cups of mixed salad greens

Preparation:

- In a large bowl, toss the tuna, beans, tomatoes, olives, and parsley until well combined.

- In a small bowl, whisk the olive oil, lemon juice, salt, and pepper until well blended.

- Drizzle the dressing over the tuna mixture and toss to coat.

- Serve the salad over the greens or with whole wheat pita bread if desired.

Nutritional Value (per serving):

- Calories: 314

- Fat: 12 g

- Carbohydrates: 25 g

- Fiber: 7 g

- Protein: 31 g

Cooking Time: 15 minutes

9. Turkey and Cheese Wrap with Lettuce and Tomato

Ingredients:

- 4 whole wheat tortillas

- 4 tablespoons of low-fat cream cheese

- 8 ounces of sliced turkey breast

- 4 lettuce leaves

- 1 tomato, sliced

- Salt and pepper to taste

Preparation:

- Spread one tablespoon of cream cheese evenly over each tortilla.

- Top each tortilla with two ounces of turkey, one lettuce leaf, and a few tomato slices.

- Season with salt and pepper if desired.

- Roll up the tortillas and cut in half.

- Serve with your favorite salsa or hot sauce if desired.

Nutritional Value (per serving):

- Calories: 263

- Fat: 8 g

- Carbohydrates: 28 g

- Fiber: 4 g

- Protein: 21 g

Cooking Time: 10 minutes

10. Vegetable and Bean Chili with Whole Wheat Tortilla Chips

Ingredients:

- 2 teaspoons of vegetable oil

- 1 onion, chopped

- 2 cloves of garlic, minced

- 1 tablespoon of chili powder

- 1 teaspoon of cumin

- 1/4 teaspoon of salt

- 1/4 teaspoon of cayenne pepper (optional)

- 2 cups of vegetable broth

- 2 cans of diced tomatoes, undrained

- 2 cans of black beans, drained and rinsed

- 1 cup of corn kernels, fresh or frozen

- 1/4 cup of fresh cilantro, chopped

- 8 whole wheat tortillas, cut into wedges

- Cooking spray

- Salt to taste

Preparation:

- In a large pot, heat the oil over medium-high heat. Add the onion and garlic and cook, stirring, for about 15 minutes or until soft and golden.

- Stir in the chili powder, cumin, salt, and cayenne pepper if using and cook for another minute, stirring constantly.

- Add the broth, tomatoes, beans, and corn and bring to a boil. Reduce the heat and simmer, uncovered, for about 20 minutes or until the chili is slightly thickened.

- Stir in the cilantro and keep warm.

- Preheat the oven to 375°F and lightly grease a baking sheet.

- Arrange the tortilla wedges in a single layer on the prepared baking sheet and spray with cooking spray. Sprinkle with salt if desired.

- Bake for 10 minutes or until crisp and golden.

- Serve the chili with the tortilla chips and your favorite toppings, such as low-fat cheese, sour cream, or avocado.

Nutritional Value (per serving):

- Calories: 366

- Fat: 7 g

- Carbohydrates: 64 g

- Fiber: 16 g

- Protein: 16 g

Cooking Time: 45 minutes

DINNER RECIPES FOR LIVER DISEASE

1. Salmon with Quinoa and Broccoli

Ingredients:

- 4 salmon fillets (about 4 ounces each)

- 2 tablespoons of lemon juice

- Salt and pepper to taste

- 1 cup of quinoa, rinsed and drained

- 2 cups of water

- 1/4 teaspoon of salt

- 2 cups of broccoli florets

- 2 teaspoons of olive oil

- 2 cloves of garlic, minced

- 2 tablespoons of chopped parsley

Preparation:

- Preheat the oven to 375°F and lightly grease a baking dish.

- Place the salmon fillets in the prepared baking dish and drizzle with the lemon juice. Season with salt and pepper to taste.

- Bake for 15 to 20 minutes or until the salmon is flaky and cooked through.

- In a small saucepan, bring the quinoa, water, and salt to a boil over high heat. Reduce the heat and simmer, covered, for about 15 minutes or until the quinoa is fluffy and the water is absorbed. Fluff with a fork and keep warm.

- In a large skillet, heat the oil over medium-high heat. Add the broccoli and garlic and cook, stirring, for about 10 minutes or until the broccoli is crisp-tender.

- Stir in the parsley and season with salt and pepper to taste.

- Serve the salmon with the quinoa and broccoli.

Nutritional Value (per serving):

- Calories: 386

- Fat: 14 g

- Carbohydrates: 36 g

- Fiber: 6 g

- Protein: 34 g

Cooking Time: 30 minutes

2. Vegetable Lasagna with Low-Fat Cheese

Ingredients:

- 9 whole wheat lasagna noodles

- 2 teaspoons of olive oil

- 1 onion, chopped

- 2 cloves of garlic, minced

- 2 cups of sliced mushrooms

- 2 cups of spinach, chopped

- 2 cups of low-fat ricotta cheese

- 1/4 cup of grated Parmesan cheese

- 1 egg

- Salt and pepper to taste

- 2 cups of marinara sauce

- 1 cup of low-fat mozzarella cheese, shredded

Preparation:

- Cook the lasagna noodles according to the package directions, drain, and rinse under cold water.

- In a large skillet, heat the oil over medium-high heat. Add the onion and garlic and cook, stirring, for about 15 minutes or until soft and golden.

- Add the mushrooms and spinach and cook, stirring, for another 10 minutes or until the mushrooms are browned and the spinach is wilted.

- In a medium bowl, stir the ricotta cheese, Parmesan cheese, egg, salt, and pepper until well combined.

- Preheat the oven to 375°F and lightly grease a 9x13 inch baking dish.

- Spread 1/2 cup of the marinara sauce over the bottom of the prepared baking dish.

- Arrange 3 noodles over the sauce and spread half of the cheese mixture over the noodles.

- Spoon half of the vegetable mixture over the cheese and sprinkle 1/3 cup of the mozzarella cheese over the vegetables.

- Repeat with another layer of noodles, cheese, vegetables, and mozzarella.

- Top with the remaining noodles and sauce and sprinkle the remaining mozzarella cheese over the top.

- Bake for 25 to 30 minutes or until the cheese is melted and bubbly.

- Let the lasagna stand for 10 minutes before cutting and serving.

Nutritional Value (per serving):

- Calories: 325

- Fat: 11 g

- Carbohydrates: 40 g

- Fiber: 6 g

- Protein: 21 g

Cooking Time: 60 minutes

3. Roasted Chicken with Roasted Potatoes and Asparagus

Ingredients:

- 4 chicken thighs (about 1 1/2 pounds)

- 2 tablespoons of olive oil

- Salt and pepper to taste

- 1 1/2 pounds of baby potatoes, halved

- 1 pound of asparagus, trimmed

- 2 tablespoons of fresh rosemary, chopped

- 2 cloves of garlic, minced

- 2 tablespoons of lemon juice

Preparation:

- Preheat the oven to 425°F and lightly grease a baking sheet.

- Pat the chicken thighs dry with paper towels and place them on the prepared baking sheet. Drizzle with 1 tablespoon of olive oil and season with salt and pepper to taste.

- Bake for 20 minutes or until the chicken is golden and cooked through.

- In a large bowl, toss the potatoes with 1/2 tablespoon of olive oil and salt and pepper to taste.

- In another large bowl, toss the asparagus with the remaining 1/2 tablespoon of olive oil, the rosemary, garlic, and lemon juice.

- After the chicken has baked for 20 minutes, add the potatoes and asparagus to the same baking sheet and spread them around the chicken.

- Bake for another 15 to 20 minutes or until the potatoes are tender and the asparagus is crisp-tender.

- Serve the chicken with the potatoes and asparagus.

Nutritional Value (per serving):

- Calories: 456

- Fat: 22 g

- Carbohydrates: 38 g

- Fiber: 7 g

- Protein: 30 g

Cooking Time: 45 minutes

4. Beef and Vegetable Stew with Barley

Ingredients:

- 1 pound of lean beef stew meat, cut into 1-inch pieces

- 2 tablespoons of all-purpose flour

- Salt and pepper to taste

- 2 teaspoons of vegetable oil

- 4 cups of low-sodium beef broth

- 1 bay leaf

- 1/4 teaspoon of dried thyme

- 1/4 teaspoon of dried rosemary

- 1 cup of pearl barley

- 2 carrots, peeled and chopped

- 2 celery stalks, chopped

- 1 onion, chopped

- 2 cups of green beans, trimmed and cut into 1-inch pieces

- 2 tablespoons of chopped parsley

Preparation:

- In a large Ziplock bag, toss the beef with the flour, salt, and pepper until well coated.

- In a large pot, heat the oil over medium-high heat. Add the beef and cook, stirring, for about 15 minutes or until browned on all sides.

- Add the broth, bay leaf, thyme, and rosemary and bring to a boil. Reduce the heat and simmer, covered, for about an hour or until the beef is tender.

- Add the barley, carrots, celery, and onion and simmer, covered, for another 30 minutes or until the barley and vegetables are tender.

- Add the green beans and simmer, uncovered, for another 10 minutes or until the green beans are crisp-tender.

- Discard the bay leaf and stir in the parsley.

- Serve hot or cold.

Nutritional Value (per serving):

- Calories: 367

- Fat: 9 g

- Carbohydrates: 47 g

- Fiber: 10 g

- Protein: 29 g

Cooking Time: 2 hours

5. Baked Cod with Lemon and Herbs

Ingredients:

- 4 cod fillets (about 4 ounces each)

- Salt and pepper to taste

- 2 tablespoons of fresh lemon juice

- 2 tablespoons of fresh dill, chopped

- 2 tablespoons of fresh parsley, chopped

- 2 teaspoons of olive oil

- 4 lemon slices

Preparation:

- Preheat the oven to 375°F and lightly grease a baking dish.

- Season the cod fillets with salt and pepper to taste and place them in the prepared baking dish.

- Drizzle with the lemon juice and sprinkle with the dill and parsley.

- Drizzle with the olive oil and top with the lemon slices.

- Bake for 15 to 20 minutes or until the cod is flaky and cooked through.

- Serve with your favorite side dish, such as couscous and peas, or a green salad.

Nutritional Value (per serving):

- Calories: 156

- Fat: 5 g

- Carbohydrates: 3 g

- Fiber: 1 g

- Protein: 24 g

Cooking Time: 25 minutes

6. Vegetable Curry with Chickpeas and Spinach

Ingredients:

- 2 teaspoons of coconut oil

- 1 onion, chopped

- 2 cloves of garlic, minced

- 1 tablespoon of curry powder

- 1 teaspoon of cumin

- 1/4 teaspoon of salt

- 1/4 teaspoon of cayenne pepper (optional)

- 2 cups of vegetable broth

- 2 cans of diced tomatoes, undrained

- 2 cans of chickpeas, drained and rinsed

- 4 cups of baby spinach, washed and chopped

- 2 tablespoons of fresh cilantro, chopped

- 2 cups of cooked brown rice

Preparation:

- In a large pot, heat the oil over medium-high heat. Add the onion and garlic and cook, stirring, for about 15 minutes or until soft and golden.

- Stir in the curry powder, cumin, salt, and cayenne pepper if using and cook for another minute, stirring constantly.

- Add the broth, tomatoes, chickpeas, and spinach and bring to a boil.

Reduce the heat and simmer, uncovered, for about 20 minutes or until the curry is slightly thickened, stirring occasionally.

- Stir in the cilantro and serve the curry over the rice.

Nutritional Value (per serving):

- Calories: 392

- Fat: 9 g

- Carbohydrates: 64 g

- Fiber: 16 g

- Protein: 18 g

Cooking Time: 35 minutes

7. Turkey Meatloaf with Mashed Cauliflower and Green Beans

Ingredients:

- 1 pound of lean ground turkey

- 1/4 cup of whole wheat breadcrumbs

- 1/4 cup of low-fat milk

- 1 egg

- 2 teaspoons of Worcestershire sauce

- 1 teaspoon of dried oregano

- Salt and pepper to taste

- 1/4 cup of ketchup

- 1 large head of cauliflower, cut into florets

- 2 tablespoons of butter

- 2 tablespoons of low-fat cream cheese

- Salt and pepper to taste

- 2 cups of green beans, trimmed and cut into 1-inch pieces

- 2 teaspoons of olive oil

- 2 cloves of garlic, minced

- Salt and pepper to taste

Preparation:

- Preheat the oven to 375°F and lightly grease a loaf pan.

- In a large bowl, mix the turkey, breadcrumbs, milk, egg, Worcestershire sauce, oregano, salt, and pepper until well combined.

- Shape the mixture into a loaf and place it in the prepared pan. Spread the ketchup over the top of the loaf.

- Bake for 45 minutes or until the meatloaf is cooked through and the ketchup is slightly caramelized.

- In a large pot, bring some water to a boil and add the cauliflower. Cook for 15 minutes or until the cauliflower is very tender. Drain and return to the pot.

- Add the butter and cream cheese and mash the cauliflower with a potato masher or a hand mixer until smooth and creamy. Season with salt and pepper to taste.

- In a large skillet, heat the oil over medium-high heat. Add the green beans and garlic and cook, stirring, for about 10 minutes or until the green beans are crisp-tender. Season with salt and pepper to taste.

- Serve the meatloaf with the mashed cauliflower and green beans.

Nutritional Value (per serving):

- Calories: 367

- Fat: 16 g

- Carbohydrates: 32 g

- Fiber: 8 g

- Protein: 28 g

Cooking Time: 60 minutes

8. Greek Salad with Grilled Chicken and Pita Bread

Ingredients:

- 4 chicken breasts (about 4 ounces each)

- 2 tablespoons of lemon juice

- 2 teaspoons of dried oregano

- Salt and pepper to taste

- 4 cups of romaine lettuce, chopped

- 2 cups of cherry tomatoes, halved

- 1 cucumber, diced

- 1/4 cup of sliced black olives

- 1/4 cup of feta cheese, crumbled

- 1/4 cup of Greek yogurt

- 2 tablespoons of extra virgin olive oil

- 2 tablespoons of red wine vinegar

- Salt and pepper to taste

- 4 whole wheat pita breads, warmed

Preparation:

- In a small bowl, toss the chicken with the lemon juice, oregano, salt, and pepper until well coated. Refrigerate for at least 30 minutes or up to 4 hours.

- Preheat a grill or a grill pan over medium-high heat. Grill the chicken for about 15 minutes, turning once, or until cooked through and slightly charred. Transfer to a cutting board and let it rest for 10 minutes. Cut into thin slices.

- In a large bowl, toss the lettuce, tomatoes, cucumber, olives, and feta cheese until well combined.

- In a small bowl, whisk the yogurt, olive oil, vinegar, salt, and pepper until well blended.

- Drizzle the dressing over the salad and toss to coat.

- Serve the salad with the chicken and pita bread.

Nutritional Value (per serving):

- Calories: 398

- Fat: 15 g

- Carbohydrates: 38 g

- Fiber: 6 g

- Protein: 32 g

Cooking Time: 45 minutes (plus marinating time)

9. Vegetable and Tofu Stir-Fry with Brown Rice

Ingredients:

- 1 cup of brown rice

- 2 cups of water

- 1/4 teaspoon of salt

- 1/4 cup of low sodium soy sauce

- 2 tablespoons of rice vinegar

- 1 tablespoon of honey

- 1 tablespoon of cornstarch

- 1/4 teaspoon of red pepper flakes (optional)

- 2 teaspoons of sesame oil

- 1 block of firm tofu, drained and cut into 1-inch cubes

- 2 cups of broccoli florets

- 1 carrot, peeled and sliced

- 1 red bell pepper, sliced

- 2 green onions, sliced

- 2 tablespoons of sesame seeds, toasted

Preparation:

- In a small saucepan, bring the rice, water, and salt to a boil over high heat. Reduce the heat and simmer, covered, for about 40 minutes or until the rice is tender and the water is absorbed. Fluff with a fork and keep warm.

- In a small bowl, whisk the soy sauce, vinegar, honey, cornstarch, and red pepper flakes if using until well blended.

- In a large skillet, heat the oil over high heat. Add the tofu and cook, turning occasionally, for about 15 minutes or until golden and crisp.

- Transfer the tofu to a plate and keep warm.

- In the same skillet, add the broccoli, carrot, and bell pepper and stir-fry for about 10 minutes or until crisp-tender.

- Add the sauce and bring to a boil. Cook, stirring, for about 5 minutes or until the sauce is thickened and glossy.

- Return the tofu to the skillet and toss to combine.

- Serve the stir-fry over the rice and sprinkle with the green onions and sesame seeds.

Nutritional Value (per serving):

- Calories: 392

- Fat: 14 g

- Carbohydrates: 54 g

- Fiber: 7 g

- Protein: 18 g

Cooking Time: 55 minutes

10. Vegetable and Cheese Quesadillas

Ingredients:

- 4 whole wheat tortillas

- 1 cup of low-fat cheddar cheese, shredded

- 1/4 cup of salsa

- 1/4 cup of black beans, drained and rinsed

- 1/4 cup of corn kernels, fresh or frozen

- 2 tablespoons of chopped cilantro

- Cooking spray

- 1/4 cup of low-fat sour cream

Preparation:

- Preheat a large skillet over medium-high heat and lightly spray with cooking spray.

- Place one tortilla on the skillet and sprinkle 1/4 cup of cheese over half of the tortilla.

- Spoon 1 tablespoon of salsa, 1 tablespoon of beans, 1 tablespoon of corn, and 1/2 tablespoon of cilantro over the cheese.

- Fold the other half of the tortilla over the filling and press lightly to seal.

- Cook for about 3 minutes per side or until the cheese is melted and the tortilla is golden and crisp.

- Transfer to a cutting board and cut into wedges.

- Repeat with the remaining tortillas and fillings.

- Serve the quesadillas with the sour cream and more salsa if desired.

Nutritional Value (per serving):

- Calories: 287

- Fat: 9 g

- Carbohydrates: 38 g

- Fiber: 6 g

- Protein: 15 g

Cooking Time: 20 minutes

CONCLUSION

Liver disease is a grave illness that impacts millions of individuals globally. It may result in symptoms like edema, jaundice, exhaustion, and stomach ache. It can result in problems such liver cancer, cirrhosis, and liver failure if untreated.

Thankfully, dietary and lifestyle modifications can help prevent and treat liver disease. You will find more than fifty delectable and healthful recipes in this cookbook that are specifically created for those who suffer from liver disease. These meals are high in fiber, protein, and antioxidants and low in fat, sugar, and sodium. They also contain things like milk thistle, turmeric, garlic, and green tea, which are known to enhance liver health.

By following this cookbook, you will enhance your general health and liver function in addition to enjoying delicious meals. Additionally, you'll lessen your chance of experiencing more liver problems and damage. Recall that your liver is one of your body's most important organs and that it merits your consideration and care.

We sincerely hope that this cookbook has encouraged you to switch to a diet that is beneficial to your liver. If you adhere to the main ideas and tips in this book, you can also experiment with your own recipes. You will quickly learn that maintaining a healthy diet for your liver is not only advantageous but also pleasurable and fulfilling.

We appreciate you selecting this cookbook, and we hope your path to a happier and healthier liver is filled with success.

We are very grateful that you have purchased this **Non-Alcoholic Fatty Liver Disease cookbook,** and we hope that it has helped you improve your health and well-being. We would love to hear your feedback and suggestions on how we can make this cookbook even better for you and other readers.

If you have enjoyed this cookbook and found it useful, please consider leaving a positive review on the platform where you bought it. Your review will help us reach more people who are looking for guidance and support on how to eat well for their liver. It will also motivate us to create more quality content for you in the future.

To leave a review, simply go to the product page of this cookbook and click on the "Write a review" button. You can rate the cookbook from one to five stars, and write a few sentences about what you liked or disliked about it. You can also share your favorite recipes, tips, or success stories with other readers.

Your review will make a huge difference for us, and we appreciate your time and effort. Thank you for choosing this **Non-Alcoholic Fatty Liver Disease cookbook**, and we hope to hear from you soon.

Printed in Great Britain
by Amazon